PEBBLES
of
WISDOM

Discovered,
Uncovered,
Collected
and
Shared

by
John Chuchman

*This Book is dedicated to all the people
who knowingly or unknowingly*

*gave me,
led me to, and
helped me find*

Pebbles of Wisdom

on my journey.

*On my journey
I have been guided by many
people,
events, and
readings;
wisdom pebbles left by others
along my path
and
uncovered in my own back yard.*

*I've picked up
a number of these wisdom pebbles
glistening in the light of awareness
and I'd like to share their beauty with you.*

*I recognize that you might not think them
all beautiful or useful,
but on the chance that some may attract you
and help you along the way,
I share them with Love.*

*I throw them into
The Lake of Life
not knowing how far the ripples will travel,
some skipping along the water
numerous times
before sinking in,
others dropping in "gerplunk"
then sinking deeply quickly.*

PEBBLES

*Along my journey,
I found some wisdom pebbles;
I share them with you.*

*Along my journey,
I mined some wisdom pebbles;
I share them with you.*

*Along my journey,
I saved some wisdom pebbles;
I share them with you.*

*Use them as you wish;
Admire them as jewels
or firm your footing.*

*Use them as you wish;
Throw them back into life's lake,
watching ripples flow.*

*Along our journeys,
we share wisdom pebbles,
along our journeys.*

. . . The Adventure

is just beginning . . .

*I've discovered that
the answers are all around me;
It's the right questions
that are difficult to find.*

*The Grandeur of Man
does not lie in his cunning cleverness
for titanic creations,
but resides most of all
in the Incredible Power
To Empty himself of himself,
To Grow beyond childhood and the false self,
To Participate in that state of
Spiritual Poverty and Emptiness
which permits him to Experience
Ultimate Reality.*

The way to Enlightenment

*is not to use the imagination
in search of Light;*

*It is
to make the darkness in us
Conscious,*

*to expose it
to the Light.*

*Just as the lake
best reflects the sky
when Calm;*

*So you
best reflect God,
when Quiet.*

That which is the most Personal;
That which is Deep within us
is the most Universal.

Sharing with Others
the very Personal which is Deep within us
is the way we truly Connect
to Others,
to all of Humanity,
and likely, to God.

To be a person is a gift.

*To give
that gift to someone
is
to receive the gift
of being a Person.*

*I revel in Creation's beauty
and am energized.*

*I Love
and most times
the beloved accepts my Love
(except when feeling unlovable)
and is energized by it.*

*Accepted or not,
Loving
taps me into the Source of all energy
and
I am energized.*

*You don't show your love
for those around you
by becoming a person they want you to be.*

You show your love for others

*by becoming the person
You want to be,
the person God wants you to be.*

*Only then,
can you truly love them.*

*God wants you to be
Who He created you to be.*

*Why do you let others
make you into who they want you to be?
Why do you let those around you
create and define you
and thus frustrate God's plan for you?*

*You will only be truly happy
when you become
Who He created you to be;
when you let yourself become
Who you want to be: His image of you.*

*God creates you;
has a Divine plan for you;
Loves you.*

*Why do you, instead, choose
others' plans for you?
Why do you let others selfishly define
and create you?
Why not become the person
God Loves you to be?*

*Only by becoming the person
He has Lovingly created;
Only by fulfilling His Divine plan for you,
can you be happy,
can you truly Love others.*

I Peter 4, 10-11

*God has given each of you
some special abilities.
Be sure to use them to help each other,
passing on to others
God's many kinds of Blessings.*

*Are you called to Preach?
Then Preach as though God Himself
were Preaching
through you.*

*Are you called to help others?
Then do it with all the strength and energy
that God supplies
so that God will be Glorified through Jesus
Christ.*

I Peter, 1, 22

Now, you can have real Love for Everyone

*Because your souls have been cleansed
from selfishness and hatred*

When you Trusted Christ

to save you.

*The decision to accept Christ
as the revelation of God's plan for the world is
an inexorable renunciation of
any attempt to live on two levels at once:
One a Sacred level, the level of the Soul,
of Spirituality, Recollection and Goodness;
The other a material level of work,
distraction, recreation, politics, etc.,
all of it real enough,
but unrelated to what goes on
in my interior castle.
If Christ is the revelation of
the meaning of life,
everything in my life becomes
relevant or irrelevant
as it tends to my growth as a Child of God.*

*The world we perceive through our senses,
the whole gorgeous and terrible pageant,
is like the breath thin surface
of a bubble.*

*Everything else,
inside and out,
is pure radiance.*

*Both Suffering and Joy
come then like a brief reflection*

and

death

like a pin.

*The Bereaved
won't care
How much I know
until they know
How much I Care.*

St. Thomas Aquinas says that

*Fear flows out of Love;
We only fear whatever threatens
what we Love.*

*If I Love success, status, control,
possessions, wealth, acquisitions,
Then I fear their loss.
But, if I Love myself and God,
Who cannot be threatened,
there is no place for fear in my life.*

*When we pray,
We are not to ask for what we desire.
At Cana, Mary simply said,
"They have no wine."
Lazarus' sisters simply said,
"Tell the lord he is sick."*

*The Lord knows better than we
what it is we need.
The Lord is full of Compassion when He sees
the needs of a loving soul full of resignation.
We avoid pride and possessiveness
by simply exposing what we lack
rather than what we think we need.*

*Dear God,
Please help us to understand and accept
your invitation in the Sermon on the Mount
to be Blessed in Mourning for
the Beloved we have lost.
The pain, sorrow, anguish,
The anger, fear, guilt and
loneliness that we feel
are not in themselves good;
in fact, they are terrible.
But Feeling those Feelings and
Expressing them in Holy Mourning for our
Lost Loved-ones
are Necessary, Normal and Healthy and
a Tribute due to the ones we have lost.
And they form the gates through which
We will receive Comfort,
from others, from within ourselves and
from You.*

*The Spiritual is not the religious.
Religion is dogma, a set of beliefs
about the Spiritual,
and a set of practices
arising out of those beliefs.
Many religions seek to be exclusive,
tending to think they have the dibs on
the Spiritual,
believing that their way is the only way.*

*The Spiritual is Inclusive, not exclusive.
It is the deepest sense of Belonging and
Participation.
The Spiritual is a realm of experience
to which
religion attempts to connect us
through dogma and practice.
Sometimes it succeeds, sometimes it fails.*

*Religion can be a bridge to the Spiritual,
But the Spiritual lies beyond religion and
rather than separating people,
Spirituality unites us all.*

While the Breath of God,
His Holy Spirit, the Wind
cools, refreshes and renews me
aflame with Love,
That very Breeze
fans the fire within me and
increases the blaze that consumes me,
ultimately uniting me with my Love,
God.

*Just as we grieve the loss of a Loved-One,
We grieve the loss of our freedom
at the hands of an addiction.*

*Just as we temporarily deny
the loss of a Loved-One,
So too, when we lose our freedom
to an addiction,
do we tend to deny that loss . . .*

Until we choose to free ourselves again.

COMPASSION

*Not pity, but Celebration
Not sentiment, but Justice and Mercy
Not private, but Public
Not solely human, but Cosmic and Divine
Not ascetic, nor abstract, but Passionate and Caring
Not anti-intellectual,
but Seeking to Understand
Not religious, but A Way of Life
Not a commandment, but A Flow of Human/Divine Energy
Not altruism, but Self-Love and Other-Love together*

The Fullest Expression of Spirituality

The Caring Paradox

*My self-realization has been possible only
through Caring for others.*

*Caring for and about others has meant Caring
for myself.*

*Caring for others has brought me great gifts:
It has increased my self-esteem;
It has attracted
the Care and Concern of others;
It has helped improve the Quality of Life.
Caring has been double-edged:
I have had an impact on others
by acknowledging their impact on me;
I have grown
by supporting the growth of others.*

MINISTRY

A Response to Need

*Discerning Needs,
Then Listening and Responding to them
in the Light of the Gospel.*

No realm of life is excluded from Ministry.

*Nurturing Life and Goodness;
Combating Evil.*

I know that I must Love.

I don't know fully what that means.

I pray daily for God's help.

FORGIVENESS
(The path from hurt to healing)

1. Feel the pain
(A thing buried alive comes up elsewhere.)
2. Take it to the Lord.
(Talk it out.)
3. Make a choice to forgive.
(God will take it from the head to the heart.)
4. Listen to the Holy Spirit.
(She will instruct you.)
5. Be open to the excusing factor.
(They did not know what they were doing.)
6. Receive inner healing.
7. Go the extra mile to pray for them.
(for those things you want for yourself)

What another can say as well as you;
Do not say it.

What another can write as well as you;
Do not write it.

What another can do as well as you;
Do not do it.

Find and Be Faithful to that which exists
Nowhere, but in you
and
Say it, Write it, Do it.

Christian Minister of Today

- *Articulator of Inner events*
(Create space for him.)
(Offer yourself as a source for clarification.)

- *Compassionate*
(Free yourself from restrictive shame.)
(Bring out the Best in others.)

- *Contemplative*
(Take away the illusory mask of the manipulative world.)
(Look for Hope and Promise in any situation.)

HEALING

*Evoking in another
The Will to Live*

by Listening,

*thus convincing them,
that they, their experience, their suffering
Matter.*

The Past is Forgiven;

The Future is Certain;

The Present is Pleasant.

If not now,

When?

*Until one is Committed,
there is hesitancy, the chance to draw back,
ineffectiveness.*

*Concerning acts of initiative and creation,
there is one elementary Truth,
the ignorance of which kills
countless ideas and plans:*

*THE MOMENT ONE DEFINITELY
COMMITS ONESELF
THEN PROVIDENCE MOVES TOO.*

*All sorts of things occur to help one
that would never otherwise have occurred.
A whole stream of events
issues from the decision,
raising in one's favor all manner of
unforeseen incidents
and meetings and material assistance
which no one could have dreamt would come
their way.*

*WHATEVER YOU CAN DO OR DREAM
YOU CAN DO, BEGIN IT.
Boldness has Genius, Power, and Magic in it.*

Begin it NOW!

Fear is in the Future.

Peace is in the Present.

The Past is past.

GRACE

*is the ultimate depth of everything we do
in our daily ordinary lives:
birth, suffering, courage, failure, hope, death.*

Grace
is the Spiritual depth of everything we do
when we realize ourselves in God's image;
when we laugh and cry, accept responsibility,
love,
live and die, stand up for truth,
refuse to be self-preoccupied,
serve our neighbors,
hope against hope,
refuse to be embittered by
the stupidities of daily life,
keep silent (not so that evil festers in the heart,
but so that it dies there),
when we live as we wish
(in opposition to selfishness and despair).
All these are Grace
because they lead us to the Eternal
and the Victory that is God.

ASCETIC WAY

*A desire for God,
An Openness to the Gifts God offers us,
A Willingness to Learn and Confront
the patterns of sinfulness in our lives,
Nurtured by
A Loving, Attentive, Contemplative stance
towards the persons in our lives and
a Willingness to Walk in the others' shoes and
A Desire to be Patient and Commit to the
long haul.*

TRUTH

*is in the
coming together of*

OPPOSITES.

Dimensions of Faith

- *Belief: Assent of the mind to one's convictions*
- *Trust: Moving from the mind to the Heart*
- *Obedience: Belief and Trust translated into a Pattern of Life*
- *Hope: Moving forward in life*
- *Fidelity: Loyalty to God as I encounter Him*
- *Perseverance: Suffering the process till death*
- *Love: Allowing others to be other than as I wish.*

EMOTIONS

*The importance of emotions
does not lie in their capacity to direct
our actions wisely;
Knowing what we feel
does not prescribe what we are to do.
But, Knowing what we Feel
is an essential aspect of making
Responsible Choices.
Emotions are the true indicators of
what's going on in our Hearts.*

*In our heads
we are capable of self-justification and
rationalization;
But our stomachs do not lie.
Our Emotions are not wise, but they are True.
If unattended and denied,
they can silently hold us captive
against our will.
Emotions serve a critical diagnostic function
of Freedom.
Allowed to speak,
they contribute to the Dialogue of
Discernment
that is the mark of
True Freedom.*

*Being truly known by God
(better than we know ourselves)
provides us with the very basis of
our Freedom
to be ourselves, rather than a prisoner of
the perceptions of others.*

*It is because God is our Judge,
that our Interior Intentions matter.
Purity of Heart
is only significant because
God knows and judges our Intentions.*

SACRAMENTALITY

*The capacity of the world to Reveal
and people to Apprehend
The Mysterious Presence of God*

SACRAMENTAL REALITY

*Any reality that makes us aware of
God's Presence,
that puts us in touch with
The Awesome Mystery of God.*

*Out of His Glorious and Unlimited Resources
He will give you
the mighty Inner Strengthening of
The Holy Spirit.
Christ will be more and more at home
in your Hearts
Living within you as you Trust in Him.
Your roots will go down deep into the soil of
God's marvelous Love
And you will be able to feel and understand,
as all God's children do,
How long, how wide, how deep, how high
His Love really is.
You will experience this Love for yourselves,
though it is so Great,
You will never see the end of it or
fully know or understand it.
And so at last you will be filled
with God Himself.
God, by His mighty Power at work within us
is able to do far more than
we would ever dare to ask or dream of
"infinitely beyond"
Our highest thoughts, desires, prayers, or
hopes.*

Ephesians 4, 16-20

5 MINUTE MIRACLE

*Create a Warm Loving Atmosphere,
Relax the other.
Touch the other in a Caring way.
Ask the other for Permission to Pray Together.
Keep words Simple.
Ask the other to give God permission
to Come and Help.
Ask Jesus to Heal root causes and
bring Wholeness.
Entrust results to the Lord.
Pray the other can Listen and Trust God.
Bring Jesus to the Center of the problem.
Love, Listen, Share Without judgement.
Respect other's views.
Avoid Advising.
Pray for God's Will.
Know that you may never know results.
Hug.*

SPIRITUALITY

Seeing the face of God,

Striving to live in His Presence,

*Striving to fashion a life of Holiness
appropriate to
His Presence.*

SPIRITUALITY

Faith seeking Maturity

and thus

Growing

*Heaven is nearer to our souls than
the world is to our bodies.*

*We are created and we are redeemed to
have our conversation in it.*

*God, the only good of all intelligent natures,
is not an absent or distant God,
but is more present in and to our souls than
our own bodies.*

*We seem strangers to Heaven and
far from God
only for this reason:
because we are void of that spirit of prayer
which alone can and never fails to unite us
with the only Good and
to open Heaven and the Kingdom of God
Within us.*

Prayer is a state of continual Gratitude.

*If I do not feel a sense of Joy
in God's Creation,
If I forget to offer the world back to God
with Thankfulness,
I have advanced very little upon the way,
I have not yet learned to be truly human.*

*For it is only in Thanksgiving
that I can become myself.*

*Breathing In,
I Calm body and mind.
Breathing out,
I Smile.*

*Dwelling in the present moment,
I know this is the only moment.*

*I have found
that the very feeling which seemed to me
most private, most personal,
most incomprehensible by others,
has turned out to be an expression for which
there is a deep resonance
in many other people.*

*I now believe
that what is most personal and unique
in each of us,
if shared or expressed,
is what speaks most deeply to others,
connects us with each other, all of humanity,
and
with God.*

Earth's crammed with heaven,
and every common bush afire with God;
But only he who sees, takes off his shoes,
(The rest sit around and pick blackberries,
and daub their natural faces unaware
more and more from the first similitude.)
If one could feel,
not one day in the artist's ecstasy,
but every day, feast, fast, or working day,
the Spiritual significance burn through
the hieroglyphic of material shows,
henceforward he would pain the globe
with wings,
and reverence fish and fowl, the bull, the tree,
and even his very body as a human.

Elizabeth Barrett Browning.

*The Grace of God, pouring forth from God,
is an inward thrust and urge
of the Holy Spirit.*

*It drives our spirit from within
exciting it
toward all virtues.*

*This Grace flows from within,
and not from outside;
For God is more in us than we are ourselves.
His inward thrust, His working within us,
be it natural or supernatural,
is nearer to us and more intimate to us
than our own workings.
God works in us from within outwards;
Creatures work from without inwards.*

*It is thus that Grace and all the Gifts of God,
and even the voice of God,
come from within, in the unity of our spirit,
and not from without into the imagination
by means of sensible images.*

*Many people with a low self-image
suffer from varying degrees of self-hatred.*

This is Pride, albeit in reverse.

*These people demean themselves
because they do not measure up to
the idealized image of perfection
their own self-image demands.*

*When they fail to meet
this impossible standard,
Pride, not God, says, "You're no good."
They then feel shame
for failing to measure up
to the grandiose expectations of themselves
that their upbringing, culture, or
drive to achieve
created.*

God asks for our consent

*In Childhood – to the basic Goodness
of our Nature.*

*In Adolescence – to the full Development
of our Being
by activating our Talents and Creative
Energies.*

*In early Adulthood – to Accept the fact
of our Non-being,
Illness, Old age, Death.*

*In later Adulthood – to be Transformed,
to the Death of our False-Self.*

*In essence, to consent to
Welcome Life and Death
as God's Gracious Gifts.*

He roused my sleeping soul.

*He stirred and softened and wounded
my Heart,
for it was hard and stony and poor in health.*

*He began, too, to pluck out and destroy,
to build up and to plant,
to water and to dry places,
to lighten the dark corners,
to throw open the closed doors,
to enkindle the chilled regions,
to make the crooked straight and
the rough places plain,
so that my soul blessed the Lord
and all that was within me praised the Lord.*

TO REPENT

*is NOT to take on afflictive penances
like fasting, vigils, flagellation.*

To Repent

*is to Change the Direction
in which
We are Looking for Happiness.*

*The world is imprisoned
in its own activity,*

*except when
actions are performed as
Worship to God.*

*Therefore, perform every action
Sacramentally
and be free from all attachment to
results.*

CIRCLES

include everyone on an equal basis
(no head, nor foot, no beginning, no end).
are Complete in any size.
are Safe and Secure
(once closed, no intrusion).
are Historical, Mythical, Spiritual
(Zen: Nothing, yet Complete)
(Native American).
provide nothing behind which to hide
(tables, desks, etc.).
allow each to See All, to See Each.

What can a person do to earn his birth?

*Is it better to imagine and think about God
or keep still in peace and quiet
so God can speak and act in me while
I merely wait on God's operation?*

*The best and utmost attainment in this life
is to remain still and let God speak in me.*

*When my bodily powers
have been withdrawn,
then is the word spoken.*

*The more completely
I can draw in my faculties
and forget the things to which I am attached,
the nearer and more susceptible I am
to God's word.*

MYSTICAL PRAYER
has nothing to do with words and petitions.

It is not articulate,
It has no form.
It is nothing else, but a Yearning of the Soul.

Mystical Prayer is the Uniting of the Soul
with God
without the intervention of the imagination
or reason,
but only with a simple attention of the mind
and
a Humble Self-Forgetting action of the Will.

To see a world in a grain of sand

and heaven in a wild flower;

Hold infinity in your hand

and eternity in an hour.

*THE WAY OF GROWTH
lies through a gradual increase in
impersonality
by an ever deeper and more intense unifying
of the self with a greater than itself.*

*In this process,
Prayer, Worship, Meditation,
Philosophy, Art, Literature
all play their part
since all help in purifying the inner being and
disposing it more and more for contact with
the Divine.*

To reach God

is to enter into

One's Self.

*He who inwardly enters and intimately
penetrates into himself
gets above and beyond himself*

and truly reaches up to God.

The Eye

with which I see God

*is the same eye
with which*

God sees me.

CATHOLIC MYSTICAL THEOLOGY

*The Godhead is absolute stillness and rest,
free of all activity and inaccessible to
human thought,
yet alive through and through,
A tremendous Energy pouring itself
out onto the world
and drawing that world back into itself.*

*There is complete unity in everything;
All is in God and God is in all.*

Man's real self is Divine.

*Truth is within ourselves;
It takes no rise from outward things,
whatever you believe.*

*There is an innermost center in us all
where Truth abides in fullness
and wall upon wall, the gross flesh hems it in,
this perfect clear perception which is Truth.
A baffling and perverted carnal mesh binds it
and makes all error.*

*To Know rather consists in
opening out a way
whence the imprisoned splendor may escape,
than in effecting entry for a light
supposed to be without.*

*In order to have pleasure in everything,
Desire to have pleasure in nothing.*

*In order to possess everything,
Desire to possess nothing.*

*In order to be everything,
Desire to be nothing.*

*In order to know everything,
Desire to know nothing.*

*When your mind dwells upon anything,
you stop seeking ALL.*

*In order to move from all to ALL,
you must deny yourself all.*

St. John of the Cross

*I want, first of all, to be at Peace with myself.
I wish a singleness of eye,
a purity of intention,
a central core to my life that will enable me to
carry out obligations and activities
as well as I can.
I want, in fact, to borrow from
the language of the Saints:
to live in Grace
as much of the time as possible.*

*By Grace, I mean inner harmony,
essentially Spiritual,
which can be translated
into outward harmony,
essentially Spiritual,
which can be translated into
outward harmony.*

*I seek perhaps what Socrates sought
when he said,
"May my Outward and Inward Man
be at One.*

*Every Human and Animal
is born with a certain number of days
to their Circle.*

*Some lives are long,
others are short,*

But all are Complete.

MYSTICISM

*The deep personal conviction,
born of personal experience,
that the divine exists deep within all of us*

and

*that it is our true lifelong goal
to come in contact with that Divinity.*

MIRACLE HOUR

(Five minutes each)

Praise
Sing
Warfare
Surrender

Holy Spirit
Repentance

Forgiveness
Scripture
Listen

Intercessions.
Petitions

Thanksgiving

PRAYING

*is like facing a large field
newly covered with snow*

*and asking,
"where is the path?"*

*Walk across it,
and then
There will be a path.*

*All I have
I'll leave behind.*

*All I am,
I'll take with me.*

*Take a Prayer, Song, and Stone with you
on your journey.
The prayer you can call on in times of need.
It can ground you and bring you Courage.
Prayer will be a Guide and Companion
along the way.*

*The Song will move you deeply.
It will fill your heart with Joy and Hope.
It will bring Peace and
Compassion to your soul.
Every heart has an ear for music,
the language of all,
not limited by distance or time.*

*A smooth Stone will be your Reality Check.
It will be your reminder to live in the Now.
The touchstone can be held through
long nights and difficult days.*

The only things worth having

*are those things which grow
when shared with others.*

*Our gold, silver, diamonds, etc. diminish
when shared with others.*

Our Ideas, Love, Trust, Loyalty, etc. grow

when shared.

These alone are worth having.

*There is no lack of Spiritual Guidance in life,
only a lack of awareness of
the Guidance being given.*

God is guiding us every moment of the day;

we need only be Aware and Open.

SPIRITUAL LIFE

*is a powerful, fast-moving stream
of living waters.*

*We can choose to jump in and live it
(without knowing how deep it is or
where it will take us)
and risk drowning
or
We can simply choose to watch it go by
and stay high and dry
without risk along the bank.*

*(We know the fresh clear waters taste good,
but
we can't get enough from the bank.)*

*We Suffer
when we want the moment to be
other than it is.*

*The desert can be a paradise
if we accept it as it is
rather than wishing it to be
other than it is.*

*The only difference
between
STEPPING STONES
and
STUMBLING BLOCKS
is*

How we use them.

God's Love for us

is no greater in Heaven

than it is for us

right Here and Now.

For Today, Be Silent.

Use words wisely . . . if at all.

*Speak only
if you can improve upon the Silence.*

*Say Nothing;
Become like a rock.*

*I shall be Silent, Slow-Paced
as warm morning Sunshine*

on a rock.

MEDITATION

*is being
Present, Open, Awake

neither clinging to,

nor rejecting

Anything.*

Tell me what you think,
and I may be able to categorize you.

Tell me what you feel,
and I can get to know you.

*Move into the Center of your Soul
where God speaks and you hear and
receive His Word.*

*You have to go into Silence and Solitude;
You have to Meditate and hope that
Meditation will lead to prayer.
In that prayer, You hear God speak.*

*Then God commands you
to do something significant
that only you can do
which will make all the difference
in the apocalyptic warfare:*

*Whether or not Christ Prevails over Satin
and the power of earth.*

*An Eye of God
(Native American Wall Hanging)
is like life.
It begins with God at the center,
and then we weave in our own colors,
our own patterns
to make it uniquely ours.
In the making,
we know not
how the completed work will appear;
It seems to change with every stand we add.
Sometimes we forget about the Eye itself,
But when our work is finished,
we see that all of our effort,
all our weaving, all our colors,
are destined simply
to adorn the Eye
and Praise God.*

*Every day I pray
to do His Will,
to Love, to Heal in His Name,
to Grow in Faith
and to Help others find Him.*

And every day, He answers, "Yes"!

*Every day, He finds me someone to Love.
Every day, He connects me with someone
who needs some healing.
Every day, He grows my faith.
Every day,
someone I touch grows closer to Him.*

*Every day,
He allows me to do His Will*

Every day.

*Sisters and Brothers, let's Love one another,
for Love is of God.
Everyone who Loves is God's child . . . knows God
as Father.
The loveless person knows nothing of God,*

for God is Love.

God shows His Love for us

by sending us His Only son

*so that through Him we may live forever.
True Love is not us Loving God,
but God Loving us*

*by sending us His Only Son
to Atone for our sins.
Sisters and Brothers, if He Loves us so,
We must Love each other in the same way.
None of us has seen God,
but when we Love one another,
God lives in us, God's Love is perfected in us.
God's living in us and we in Him is
confirmed by the Holy Spirit.*

*We know and testify that
the Father sends His Son
to save the world*

*and when anyone acknowledges that
Jesus is Son of God,
God lives in him and he in God.
We now know and rely on God's Love for us.
When we live in Love, we live in God*

and God in us.

*Life is not a matter of arriving or
accomplishing.
Life is the traveling, the sailing.
The speed at which I travel and the tack I sail
are only partly the result of what I do.
God's winds provide my power
and often the winds in life change.
(How or why is not up to me.)
And when they change, I must change,
for I cannot continue to do the same thing
and stay on-course.
In life, I sail with winds
from North and South,
in rough seas and mild
and when I hit the doldrums,
I know it's God's way of reminding me
He's in control
and a New Wind is coming.*

The Four-fold way

Be a WARRIOR.
Show up; Choose to be present;
Access Human Power, Presence, Communication.
LEAD.

Be a HEALER.
Pay attention to what has Heart and Meaning;
Access Human Gratitude, Love, Acknowledgement.
BE HEALTHY and WHOLE.

BE A VISIONARY
Tell the Truth without blame or judgement;

Access Inner Vision, Authenticity, Intuition.
BE CREATIVE.

BE A TEACHER.
Be Open to outcome, but not attached to it;
Access Wisdom and Objectivity.
COMMUNICATE.

Death is not the opposite of Life.

Death is the opposite of birth.

Both are part of Life.

EFFECTIVE CONVERSATION

*Silence your inner critic (Suspend Judgement)
Begin with Obvious (Focus on the other)*

LISTEN

Compliment (Carefully)

LISTEN

*Use Body-friendly language
(Smile, Eye Contact, Open)
Spotlight Other*

*LISTEN
(Accept Silence, then Ask again)*

Don't take yourself too seriously (Humor)

LISTEN

*Have a Sense of Humor
Exit (Know when)*

CONVERSATION
Accomplished through Words

DIALOG
*Accomplished through the Moments of Silence
in-between the Words.*

*Behind every Sexual desire
is a very natural longing
that is not really physical.*

*It is the longing of trying to escape
the loneliness of separate existence.*

*The closer we learn to connect
with other people,
the less we will be driven for
the physical urge for sex,
for the urge will be fulfilled
much closer to its source.*

*As we deepen our relationships
far below the physical level,
the sexual drive will be transformed naturally
into a dynamo of creative power,
the Power to Help,
the Power to Love.*

*The Picture Window
looking out at Torch Lake and beyond
is truly God's easel.*

*Through it,
moment by moment,
brushstroke by brushstroke,
He paints for me
an ever-changing world of Beauty.*

*Each moment,
He presents for me a picture
which was never seen before
and
which shall never be seen again.
I add each of them to my soul's collection
simply by stopping*

*and by seeing
and by Rejoicing.*

So he returned home to his father.

*And while he was still a long distance away,
his father saw him coming and was filled with
Love
and ran and embraced him and kissed him*

(even before he knew his son was repentant).

*His son said,
Father I have sinned against Heaven and you,
and am not worthy of being called your son."
But his father said,
"We must celebrate with a feast,
for this son of mine was dead and
returned to life;
He was lost and is found."*

Prayer before Communion

*Dear God, I offer myself to you.
Please accept me
with all my faults and imperfections.
You created me perfect in Your Image,
but along life's way
I chose many things that served to separate us.
Please accept me with gratitude
for all the gifts you have given me,
my skills, talents, blessings.
I offer myself to you
seeking Forgiveness, Cleansing, Anointing,
Reconsecration and Rededication
to Your Will.
I ask this in Jesus' Name.
Amen.*

A PRAYER

(nothing)

simply standing before God with empty hands
. . .

Plant Trees

When you plant trees,

you're entitled to believe that

you'll live forever.

*How great, how great, is the difference between
the Secret Friend and the Hidden Child?*

The Friend makes Loving, living, measured ascent

towards God.

*The Child presses on to lose his own life upon the summits
in a simplicity which knows not itself.*

*And when we transcend ourselves and become so simple
that Supreme Love can lay hold on us,
then we cease and our selfhood dies in God.
In this death we become Hidden Children of God
and find New Life within us.*

*At the summit of Spiritual Knowledge,
what I know is that I know Nothing.*

But at least, I know it!

*In that Knowing is complete Trust
that I will be led from state to state,
from miracle to miracle.
I know that I am being led
by the Mysterious Hand of the Divine
and that Hand will always Guide
and Help me.
The consequences of my action,
I cannot know.
God's ultimate nature, I cannot know.
However profound my immersion in
the Peace of God,
there will always be a dimension of God
which remains beyond my comprehension.*

*I am a child dazzled by
Love, Happiness, Grace, Joy, Serenity,
Delight.*

*In every single contact
with another human being,
we will either enhance or diminish
the other person's self-esteem.*

*With each contact,
we will also either grow or diminish
our sense of self-worth.*

*But, it is not possible
to grow our own self-esteem
while diminishing an other's.
Nor can we diminish ours
by enhancing the other's.*

TRUE CONTEMPLATION

*by its very nature reaches out to others
in Compassion,
the fruit of Love and the highest expression of Love.*

*It finds its authenticity in Service,
in the care of the needs of others,
be they physical, psychological, or spiritual.*

*A contemplation that reposes
in its own isolation is
by every legitimate Christian yardstick,
a counterfeit contemplation
unworthy of the name,
Contemplation, the gift of the Holy Spirit,
impels us by that same Spirit
to reach out to others.*

LIVE

*Open your "i" (eye)
to the "O" (oh)
in awe of creation*

&

LOVE

*Immature Love says,
"I love you because I need you."*

*Mature Love is not driven by need;
It is an overflowing of Inner Richness and Joy
and is Unconditional.*

FAITH

Acceptance of the insecurity in life.

HOPE

The inner search for meaning in that insecurity.

*The Lord has given me a well-trained tongue
that I may know how to speak to the weary
a word that will rouse them.*

*Morning after morning,
He opens my ear that I may Hear
and I have not rebelled;
I have not turned back.*

Isaiah

SPIRITUALITY

Harmony

With Self

With Others
With Mother Earth
With God

*How can I hope to learn
to sail the Holy Spirit's tack,
unless I hoist the sails of my Listening
to let Her Breath propel me
through the seas of life.*

Insecurity and Self-doubt

are constant companions on my journey.

They encourage me to seek

boundaries instead of Horizons.

I thought I knew myself.

*All I knew was
what I thought about myself.*

GLORY

that does not

GLORIFY

becomes

an intolerable burden.

PRAYER

A quality of Attention to the given,

making room for

the given to appear as a Gift.

Nothing is worth anything

except
the Uncovering and Enacting
of our Divine Self.

Everything else is
evasion, frivolity, self-parody, self-destruction.

To know and Love our Divine Selves
is the only reason we are here.

SPIRITUAL HEALING

*makes use of a Prayerful, Meditative
state of Awareness;
It involves a state of Being rather than doing.*

*One can be fully in this mode when
one has – if only for a moment – given up
all wishes and desires for oneself
(as the separate self does not exist)
and even for others
(as they do not exist as separate, either)
and simply allows oneself
To Be in the Present Moment
and thus
To Be With and To Be One
with All of Existence.*

*Caring for the Bereaved requires,
not only great Sensitivity and Patience,
but also a robust and earthy Sense of Humor,*

*for in Grief,
Tragedy and Farce are inexorably
intertwined.*

*There is a deeply Contemplative aspect of
caring for the Bereaved,
for it demands that
we NOT DO SOMETHING for people,
but that we simply*

*BE WITH THEM
in their Grief.*

*It is a Ministry of Presence,
a being alongside them,
impotent as they are impotent,
mute as they are mute,
Sharing their Darkness.*

*The Foot-of-the-Cross Ministry
is enormously demanding
because, not only does it expose us
to the pain of others,
but it also turns the spotlight*

*on our own weaknesses.
The hardest thing about caring for the
Bereaved
is recognizing the gulf between
what I preach and practice
in that I can only sustain
the level of caring I preach
for very limited period and
only when I choose.*

*Man can try to name Love,
showering upon it
all the names at his command,
and still,
he will involve himself in self-deceptions.*

*If he possesses a grain of wisdom,
he will lay down his arms
and name the unknown
by the more unknown,
by the name of
God.*

GRIEF

does not end.

But our ego's attachment to it can end.

*On our Spiritual Journey, Grief expands
and
rather than staying personal,
it focuses on and embraces
the Grief
of all those around us.*

*The Greatness of our Hearts
lies in not demanding that our Love and Care
make a difference.*

*The Vastness of our Love
lies in not needing evidence of
the impact of our Care.*

*Our Faith in Love
itself sustains us;
The Richness of our Caring
itself nurtures us.*

*In not seeking confirmation, approval,
reward,*

*we are Free
to live simply in the Spirit of Reverence and*

Love.

*Trade with the gifts God has given you.
Bend your minds to Holy Learning
that you may escape
the fretting moth of loneliness of mind
which would wear out your souls.*

*Brace your Wills to Action
that they may not be the spoil of weak desires.
Raise your Hearts and Lips in Song
which gives Courage to the Soul.
Buffeted by trials, Learn to Laugh.
Rebuked, Give Thanks.
Having failed, Determine to Succeed.*

What is to Give Light

must endure Burning.

*I am not special,
quite ordinary,
but I know that I am Loved by God.*

*We are all ordinary,
born in littleness and called to die in littleness.*

*But, we are all Loved
and
We all have a Mission
To Love.*

Mother Teresa's SIMPLE PATH begins in Silence.

*The Fruit of Silence is Prayer
(What we say to God is not so important
as what He says to us – when we Listen.)
The Fruit of Prayer is Faith
(When we empty ourselves, He fills us.)
The Fruit of Faith is Love.
(When we are filled with Love,
it emanates from us.)
The Fruit of Love is Service.
(Our God Love manifests itself
in Service to others.)
The Fruit of Service is Peace.
(In Serving others, we find True Peace.)*

Mother Teresa's SIMPLE PATH ends with Peace.

The Native American Threefold Way

Tell the Truth.
(Put Mind, Mouth, Heart in line.)

Take Risks.
(Dare to Look at things Differently.)

Connect with others.
(No one makes it alone.)

*We must not stop at the surface
but enter ever deeper into our Divine Being
through Recollection.*

*We must descend daily
this pathway of the abyss*

which is God.

*Let us slide down this slope
in Wholly Loving Confidence.
It is there, in the very depths, that the Divine
Impact takes place,
where the abyss of our nothingness
encounters the abyss of Mercy,
the Immensity of the All of God.*

*All Creative Growth
in the second half of life (a mid-life face-lift)
has the potential to make us
Radiantly Beautiful.*

*The created self,
unrepeatable in its being
is called forth in Christ
with its own special potential for
Divinization.*

*Sent into the temporal order,
so as to be Glorified Eternally,
each person mirrors the Beauty of the Creator
in a Singular Manifestation.*

*Giving the unconscious parts
of our personality
permission to become
an active and equal part of our conscious life
puts our feet squarely on the path to
Individuation:
the road to Freedom
where we shed the image of the false self
and discover more and more
the self we were born to become:
Our True Self,
made in the image and likeness of God.*

SPEAK ONLY IF

Your words are the truth,

*It is necessary to speak them
(Do they help someone?)
(Do they clarify something?)*

and

*Your words are Kind.
(Are they Supportive and Loving?)*

IF NOT,

BE SILENT!

CENTRIFUGAL FORCE

*The faster I go,
the more I am thrown outward,
away from Center.*

*Only when I slow,
do I move to my Center,
to God within me.*

A SEEKER

*"is one who has been touched by God
in such a way
that
nothing else
or
no one else
will ever do.*

ENTHUSIASM

Supernatural Serenity

Shared Joy is double-Joy;

Shared Sorrow is half-Sorrow.

*What a shame
Women are now expending their energies
fighting over Rights.
Men have been fighting over Rights for
centuries,
with little to show for it,
except death and destruction.
Women have been Bastions of Love,
The True Source of humanity's Strength.
What a shame
Women would now sacrifice that strength
to be more like men.*

*All these years,
I worked so hard to be
the person others expected me to be,
for which I received little criticism.
Now,
that I am finally becoming the Man
I want to be,
the Man, I believe God wants me to be,
I am attacked.
I guess it comes with the territory.*

*It is not the Event that is important;
It is Our Response to the Event
that is Everything.*

*Every Attack is a Call for Help.
It is a call for help,
not only from the perceived attacker,
but also from ourself.
Thus, if we respond to the attack
with Love and Help,
We can Heal, not only the attacker,
but, indeed, Ourself.*

COINCIDENCE

is God's way

of

Remaining Anonymous.

*The way to guarantee that someone will
continue to wound others
is to keep him ignorant of his own wounds.*

*The wounded wounder
knows vaguely
that he has a wound somewhere,
but he can only see it when
it appears in someone else.*

*Wounding another makes the wound clear for
a
moment
and seems to move the pain of if
from inside the wounder
to
out in the world.*

Dear God,

*Please give me the Courage and Strength
to do Your Will today.*

*Help me to
Love,
Heal in your Name,
Grow in Faith
and
Help Others find You.*

This I ask in Jesus' name,

Amen.

Our Greatest Gift from God:

The Precious Present.

*The Greatest Power we possess is the Power
to Change ourselves.*

*Only Prayer, the Christ Power,
can change things for the better because
nothing else
really changes us.
As long as we remain the persons we are
we will have the same life we have now.
As soon as we change, our conditions change.
This is being Born Again.
This is raising up the Christ Power.
The Christ Power overcomes all obstacles,
puts down all power of the separation belief.
When the last shred of limitation belief
has gone,
death will be overcome too and
We will be a pillar in the Temple of God
needing to go out no more.
Adam and Eve drove themselves out
by accepting fear and doubt,
But Christ opens the gate and
Restores them/us.*

THE GREAT MULTIPLIER

Offer Him something,
anything
and
He will Multiply it
thousands and thousands of times,
just like the loaves and fishes.

But 1000 times nothing
is still nothing;
If you offer Him nothing,
the result is always nothing.

Offer God something,
anything,
Each Day.

Christ's last words on earth to us:

*"... and know that
I am with you always,
even until the end of the world."*

*(What is there that I cannot overcome
with Jesus at my side?)*

COMPASSION
and all the works born of Compassion
are themselves
Acts of Contemplation

*We can let the Pendulum of Life
stay centered and motionless
to avoid the pain and sorrow
at one end of the arc.
But, in doing so,
We'll miss all the joys and ecstasies
at the other end of the arc.
A clock whose pendulum doesn't swing
is rather useless anyway.*

*It is not necessary to make a big splash.
The beneficent ripples
flowing from a Pebble of Love
dropped into the Lake of Life
end up being just as Powerful and Pervasive
as those flowing from
a boulder.*

THE WIND

I don't know where it comes from,
nor where it goes;
But I can feel its presence; I know it's here.
I don't know where it comes from,
nor where it's taking me;
But I can feel its presence; I know it's here:
The Holy Spirit.

*I used to think
that being self-centered was wrong,
that it was being selfish.*

*I now know
that being self-centered means
achieving a balance between
the material . . . and . . . the spiritual,
the mental . . . and . . . the emotional,
the analytical . . . and . . . the creative,
the left brain . . . and . . . the right brain.*

*I now know that being self-centered
means finding one's True Self,
finding God within me.*

*I have grown up to be a Child again.
I feel like a little child,
my little hand held in the hand of God.
I feel He's guiding me, leading me,
baby step by baby step,
along my true path,
from which I've strayed so long.
His Love overwhelms me and
He Lovingly Laughs
as my eyes open wide with Awe
at every new experience and lesson
He is Teaching me.*

*There is no difficulty
that enough Love will not Conquer,
no disease that enough Love will not Heal,
no door that enough Love will not Open,
no gulf that enough Love will not Bridge,
no wall that enough Love will not Scale,
no sin that enough Love will not Redeem.*

*It makes no difference
how deeply seated the trouble,
how hopeless the outlook,
how muddled the tangle,
how great the mistake;
sufficient Realization of Love
will Dissolve it all.*

*If only I could Love enough,
I could be the Happiest and
Most Powerful being
in the world.*

*Loving another
Energizes them and
at the same time
Opens me to the Energy of the Universe,
allows me to tap into
God's Energy.*

*The Holy Spirit
does not quench my thirst;
She Inflames it.*

MASTERS
*are Masters because they give Living Proof to
the seeker
that what the seeker seeks
is Real.*

*are not weakened by weakness,
nor confused by confusion;
They do not let these name who they are.*

*Masters recognize in the seeker
that which the seeker is seeking.*

*know the ultimate secret:
That there are no secrets.*

Creativity finds God

Creativity requires Focus,
Focus on the Moment,
Focus on the Now.
Creativity excludes the past,
knows not the future.
Creativity pulls from Deep within.
Now Deep within
is
When and Where
God resides.

Be with What is

so that What is to be

may Become.

*In trying to find God,
we suffer because
we can't seem to "get there."
When all along, where we need to get
is "here," not "there."
But we can't "get here" because we're too busy
trying to "get there."*

FORGIVENESS

*Distancing ourselves from the hurt
and
Hugging the hurter.*

*A decision to accept God's Grace
to distance ourselves from the hurts
while showing Love and Mercy
to the hurter.*

*When we learn to say
"Here I am!"
in every moment,
then our God is free to command us.
Freedom occurs when we Surrender
to that ultimate Someone
who has captivated us
so that
We are Willing to Respond
to God the Father as did Jesus Christ.*

Don't fret about events.

*You don't control them
and, in any case,
they're not what's important for you.*

*What you do control is
how you react to events.*

*And that, and only that,
is what is really important for you.*

The earth should not be injured.
The earth should not be destroyed.
As often as the elements of the earth
are violated by ill treatment,
so God will cleanse them.
God will cleanse them through the sufferings,
through the hardships of humankind.
All of Creation
God gives to humankind to use.
But, if this privilege is misused,
God's Justice permits the Earth
to punish humankind.

Hildegard of Bingen, circa 1200

HAPPINESS
*is the easiest most difficult thing in the world
to obtain.*

*Easiest
because it is all around us, within us.*

*Most Difficult
because if we wish to possess it,
we may possess Nothing else.*

God

Sun

*The One Thing
we cannot look at
is the only thing
by whose light
we see everything.*

*Man
can understand everything
with the help of
everything he does not understand.*

*The Poet
only asks to get his head
into Heaven.
Others
try to get Heaven
into their heads.
It's the head that splits.*

WOW!
Enthusiasm for my Faith!

*Imagine the Enthusiasm in finding Jesus'
tomb empty and
then experiencing the Risen Lord!*

*Imagine Mary's Excitement as she recognizes
the Risen Lord in the one she thought was
the gardener!*

*Imagine once-doubting Thomas'
"My Lord and My God!"*

*Imagine the Enthusiasm of the blind man
healed by Christ!*

*Imagine the Thrill of Lazarus hobbling
out of the tomb!*

*Imagine the Excitement in the home of the
little girl
Jesus brought back to life!*

*Imagine the exhilaration
of the paralyzed man
offering his mat in the rummage sale!
Jesus Wowed People!*

*The smallest of acts
can teach us
everything
as long as
we know
Who
is providing the guidance.*

*In order to judge another Fairly,
we would have to know
all the past events that influenced the action,
all the people that the action impacted,
and how it impacted them,
and all the future consequences of the action.
No Way!
So, do not judge any other;
Leave it to the only One
who can judge Fairly,
God.
Whew,
what a Relief, what a Burden removed!*

For those Suffering

*Dear God,
Please give your children gathered here
the Courage and Strength
to fulfill Your Will as You would wish.
Help them
to feel Loved,
to be healed in Your Name,
to Grow in Faith,
and through their Suffering
to better Know You.
Amen.*

*Alone with God,
I find Freedom.
I am freed of the need to blame
and freed from whatever in the past
holds me impotent.
No longer bound by fear of failure or
the need to be what I believe pleases others,
I discover what it is
to be me.*

The loss of a Loved one

is a temporary and limited separation.

*Temporary
because it ends with our own death.*

*Limited
because it is confined to the body and senses.*

*Our soul does not lose anything
when a relative of ours dies.
Its freedom is limited in one party only,
in us, as survivors
with our souls still enclosed in our flesh.*

*Our relative who has passed to the next life
enjoys the Liberty and Power
to watch over us and obtain for us much more
than when it Loved us
from the prison of its body.*

Heartfelt Delight,
A flood of inward Warmth and Light,
Ineffable Enthusiasm, Joy, Lightness of Heart,
Profound Peace
and
The Very Essence of Blessedness and
Contentment
are the results of
Prayer in the Heart.

A GENUINE MYTH

*is not
a falsehood of the world
told by primitives.*

*It is
a true story
about the workings of God
in the human Soul*

told by Geniuses.

*The scars of initial woundedness and
of life-changing events
turn out to be
the Openings to Imagination and
the Heartfelt Experiences of Life.
When these experiences
are contained in
art, poetry, story, song, and dance,
the limits of the individual and of time
are shed
and
the Timeless Territory of the Heart and the
Imagination
Open.*

*Admit that
You do not know
where you are going.
If you do not know
where you are going,
you cannot get lost.*

*When the Artist is alive in any person,
whatever his kind of work may be,
He becomes
an Inventive, Searching, Daring,
Self-expressive creature.
He becomes Interesting to other people.
He disturbs, upsets, enlightens and
opens ways for a better understanding.
Those who are not Artists
are trying to close the book;
Artists open it and
show that there are still more pages possible.*

*Life
is not a matter of
always holding all the good cards,
but of
Playing a poor hand Well.*

Robert Louis Stevenson

*He's crossed over the bridge,
can never go back.
She's stayed put,
has not crossed,
may never.
There is a place
where they can meet
and share
and Love each other
where they are.
They each need to take some steps
to get there,
On the Bridge.*

*The channel through which the Holy Spirit
brings Truth to the world
is the Pastor, who helps teach it to the Laity,
who, in turn, translate it and put it
to work in the world.
The problem in the modern church
is that the channel is blocked.
The Pastor does not engage
in the secular world
on a day in, day out basis and
the Lay People tend to keep their Faith
in a compartment separate from
the rest of their lives.
Sunday after Sunday,
congregations sit passively like spectators
watching the entertainment up front,
missing the fact that
they should be absorbing the Truth
and Applying it to their Lives.*

*St. Paul says
The Pastor is not paid to do our work (service)
for us.
Pastors and Teachers
are to equip the saints (us) to serve,
to build the Body of the Church,
to Be the Church in the world.
Every Lay person is to be equipped
as a Minister of the Gospel.*

*While the church may seem to be experiencing
growth and prosperity,
it is failing to move people to
commitment and sacrifice.
We have substituted
an institutionalized religion
for the life-changing dynamic
of a Living Faith.
For most people, church is a building
where we assemble to worship.
Its ministries are the programs
in which we get involved;
Its mission is
to meet the needs of its parishioners;
its servants are the professional clergy
we hire to shepherd us.
When compared to
the previous generation of believers,
we seem most thoroughly
at peace with our culture,
the least adept at transforming society,
the most desperate for a meaningful Faith.*

Our raison d'etre is confused.

CHURCH

*It is like Noah's ark:
Not where the saved gather,
but where all can come
to be saved.
The stench in the ark (church)
would be unbearable
if it were not for
the storm outside.*

CHURCH

Not a building, People
Not simply a collection of people,
A New Community.
Not a hierarchy, A Community of God
A Community which will triumph

*Fan the flame of
discontent in not knowing what you want
into a Conflagration
which burns down your world
that is searching for
honor, power, acceptance, approval, security,
and wealth
and
Attain a Great Clarity and Insight
Delighting in Everything and Nothing.*

*I do dimly perceive
that while everything around me is changing,
is dying;
There is underlying everything
that is changing
A Living Power that is Undying,
A Power that Holds Everything Together,
that Creates, Dissolves, Re-Creates.
That Living, Informative Power is God.
Since everything that I see
merely with my senses
cannot or will not persist,
God alone is.
Is that Power good or evil?
I perceive it to be all good.
For in the midst of death, Life persists.
In the midst of untruth, Truth persists.
In the midst of darkness, Light persists.
I gather that God is Life, Truth, Light;
God is Love.
God is the Absolute, Eternal Good.*

Gandhi

*Like a picture puzzle of a million pieces,
my life seems made up of individual,
yet related
coincidental events.
I don't see the total picture;
I don't know how all the pieces fit together;
I begin to see portions take shape
and form and meaning.
As He carefully moves the pieces around,
fitting them together for me,
I begin to see how the moments and events
are related.
The chaos of all the loose pieces
spread out before me
begins to disappear.
I sense an order to it all.
I know now that my life is
the making of a beautiful picture;
that no piece will be missing,
and that every piece, light and dark, is needed
to complete it.*

St. Paul
You must lay aside your former life and
the old self
which deteriorates
through illusion and desire.
You must acquire a Fresh,
Spiritual way of thinking.
You must put on that New person
created in God's Image,
whose Justice and Holiness are born of Truth.

*Elijah had been reviled
as he tried to do God's will.
When he searched for meaning,
an angel told him to stand on the mountain,
for the Lord would pass by.
When Elijah did so,
there first came a strong heavy wind
that rended the mountain and
crushed the rocks,
but the Lord was not in the wind.
After the wind, there was an earthquake,
but the Lord was not in the earthquake.
After the earthquake, there was a fire,
but the Lord was not in the fire.*

*Finally, after all these phenomena,
in which Elijah had expected to find his God,
there came a tiny whispering sound,
as small as if it were nothing at all.*

In the Silence,

God revealed Himself to Elijah.

FOUNDATIONS of MEDITATION

*Faith, Childlike Wholeheartedness, Sincerity,
Genuineness,
Mindfulness (Being Present just to what is),
Holy Forgetfulness
(A willingness to forget
all that carries us away)
Compassion, Patience*

*In Meditation,
treat thoughts and distractions as if
you were on a river bank simply watching.
As boats come into view, you see them,
but nothing more.*

*Don't focus on them;
Don't draw them close,
Don't examine their detail;
Just let them go by.
Every time you return to prayer,
you make an act of will
by choosing to put yourself
in the presence of God.
That intention is what counts.*

Take the shoes off your feet;
You're on holy ground.
Going barefoot slows you down;
It helps to tame time.
You feel the grass instead of trampling over it
on your way somewhere else.
When you go slowly,
You smell the flowers,
You listen to God's bees,
You listen how mightily the birds chirp,
You see the diamond sparkles on the lake.
You can't get to heaven in a hurry,
only by slow and by stop.

*As the truest society
approaches always near to Solitude,
so the most excellent speech
finally falls into Silence.
Silence is audible to all, at all times,
in all places.
She is, when we hear inwardly,
sound when we hear outwardly.
Creation has not displaced Her,
but is her visible framework and complement.
All sounds are Her servants and purveyors,
proclaiming not only that their Mistress is,
but that She is a rare Mistress,
earnestly to be sought after.
They are so far akin to Silence that they are
but bubbles on Her surface,
which straightaway burst and
evidence the strength of the undercurrent;
a faint utterance of Silence, and then only
agreeable to our auditory nerves when they
contrast themselves with
and relieve the former.
As they do this in proportion, sounds are
heighteners and
intensifiers of the Silence, and are harmony
and
purest melody.*

*Silence is the universal refuge, the sequel to
all dull discourses and all foolish acts,
a balm to our every chagrin,
as welcome after satiety as after
disappointment.
Silence is the background which the painter
may not daub,
be he master or bungler.
However awkward a figure
we may have made in the foreground,
Silence remains ever our inviolable asylum,
where no indignity can assail,
no personality disturb us.
The orator puts off his individuality and
then is most eloquent
when most silent.
He listens while he speaks and is a hearer
along with his audience.*

*Forgiveness is an expression of Love.
It is based on acceptance.
Acceptance does not mean you like it;
it means
you are willing to let be and
get on with your life.
Lack of Forgiveness inhibits
your personal growth
by keeping you stuck.
It binds you to the situation
that you haven't forgotten
just as surely as if you were chained to it.
It takes you out of the moment,
out of the present time
and returns you to an unhappy state.
It is worse for you
than for the one you haven't forgiven
because it generates bad feelings in you
and you carry those with you all the time,
whether you're aware of it or not.*

*If you want to see the effects of Prayer,
Look in your life for its fruits.*

*Are you growing more Patient?
more Aware of Others?*

Are you Loving more?

Then, Prayer is taking hold.

*Relax.
Let God have His way.*

*Dear God,
Please help us not to dwell in the past,
especially our failings.
In knowing that You Forgive us,
we also Forgive ourselves.
Please help us not to worry about the future,
especially our material future;
By Trusting in You fully,
We know You will take care
of our earthly needs.
Please help us to live in the Present Moment,
to put the past and future aside and
to be in the Now.
In knowing that for You
there is no past or future,
we are aware that You are available for us
Here and Now
and that everything we will ever need
is available to us in the Present Moment.*

GIFTS OF AWE

*An Awakened Mysticism
Deep Ecumenism
A New Sense of History
The Return of the Artist
The Recovery of Compassion
The Redemption of Worship
An End to Same
The Prevention and Cure of Addiction
The Celebration of the Young
Letting Go
Empowerment*

GIFTS OF WISDOM

Extravagance
Interconnectivity
Expansion
Variety
Creativity
Emptiness
Justice
Beauty
Community
Sacrifice
Suffering and Resurrection
Paradox and Humor
Work

St. Paul

*There is a new rule
for those who will form the People of God:
It is to become an altogether New Creature.
The New Creation
takes place within our Consciousness
and it demands nothing less than
A Spiritual Revolution.*

*It is easy in the world
to live after the world's opinion.
It is easy in solitude
to live after our own.
The great person is the one,
who in the midst of the crowd,
keeps with perfect sweetness
the Independence of Solitude.*

A Path of Spiritual Growth

Meditate: half an hour each morning
Mantra: repetition at each opportunity
Slow Down: simplify and attend to details
Focus Attention: one-pointed full attention
Train the Senses:
Change likes/dislikes for the better
Put Others First: escape the ego prison
Read Mystics:
Draw inspiration from mystical readings
Associate with Spiritual:
Connect with soul mates

BEATITUDES

*Jettison every thing standing in the way of
finding God
and physical and spiritual realization
are yours.
If sorrow is necessary to bring you to God,
through it you will experience Him.
Be perfectly willing to allow
God's Will in your life
and you will bring your life
into harmony and success.
Think good thoughts at all times
and you will produce good effects.
Treat others better than they deserve
and God will do so for you.
Share everything with God
as the only real power
and you will become aware of God
and Heaven on earth.
Make true peace and serenity within yourself
and you will recognize God as your Father.
Overcome your lower nature
and you will rejoice with God.*

*There is nothing more illumining,
more ennobling
than to be one of a company of people
who have come together in order to
Free their Spirit
from entangling personal bonds,
Quiet their Soul by silence,
Release their aspirations by music or poetry,
Concentrate their Mind on spoken wisdom,
Open their Hearts
to all that is good, true, beautiful,
thus Tuning themselves to God.*

*Something crucial in us dies
without Ritual.*

*We become more reverent
by behaving reverently.*

*Symbols are means of Transformation;
They open the doors between the worlds
and prepare the way
for the archetypal invasion.*

*There is always more to know,
more to discover,
more to interpret
in your own experiences of life.*

*As you penetrate more and more
of reality,
Interpret it.
It is important to share the interpretation
with as many people
as can take it.*

CELESTINE PROPHECY

*Be Aware of
Mysterious Coincidences
The Longer Now
Energy in all things
Human Competition.
Tap in to the Universal Energy through Love.
Disconnect from lifelong control drama.
Obtain answers to the right questions
through people.
Relate to people,
Share the Prophecy*

*Everything comes from God.
Everything moves under His governance and Care.
Everything returns to God
in and through Jesus Christ.
Our first task is reverent Gratitude.
But, we are to express that
Gratitude in Action.
We are given both the responsibility and
power to act.
As the Lord Jesus did,
so must we act in the service of others.
It is in enactment that we find God.
But, unless we are also Contemplative,
we will miss seeing
God acting in everything around us and
in ourselves.*

The Four Paths of Creation Spirituality

SOUTH
Fall in Love at least three times a day
(Via Positiva)

NORTH
Dare the Dark (Via Negativa)

EAST
Give Birth (Via Creativa)

WEST
Be Compassionate (Via Transformativa)

*On judgement day
God will not ask
how much material wealth we had accumulated,
how many persons we controlled,
how many pleasures we had experienced.
These have no value beyond death.
God will simply ask
if we had been of service to others,
if we had touched and helped others,
if we had Loved.
These alone are the Keys to the Kingdom of God.*

Consciousness
Be Aware of the Present.
(Wholeness)
Happiness lies only within us.
(Faith)
God will see us through this.
(Spirituality)
God is everywhere.
Live Whole and Happy in the Now,
expecting, demanding, grasping nothing,
becoming Open to all things.

*To be Human
is to be resurrected into Community,
in Communion with God,
One Another,
Our Deepest Identity,
and with the
Cosmos.*

Four Basic Addictions

Intensity
Low Tolerance for boredom,
Dramatize, Sensationalize, Exaggerate
Drugs, Alcohol, Sex vs. Love

Perfection
No Tolerance for mistakes,
Vulnerability equals Weakness
Denial of Humanness vs. Excellence

Need to Know
No Surprises or things unexpected

Control
Little Trust
Knowledge vs. Wisdom
Fixation on what's not working
Magnify the negative, No trust of intuition
Negative vs. Intuition, Insight, Perception, Vision

*The Creative Word of God
gives birth to the Blessing that is Creation.
Humans bless other beings in a conscious way
with creativity and compassion.
God is in us and we are in God.
Eternal Life is now; no need to wait till death.
Spirituality is Cosmic, not introverted.
Letting go is
letting creation be the blessing it is.
Sink deeply into the ineffable depths of
the unfathomable ocean which is God.
We are sons and daughters of God
and need to let our limiting perspectives go.
Spirituality is a Growth Process.
Creativity is the work of God in us.
Compassion is the fullness
of Spiritual maturity.
Everyone is noble, royal, dignified and
responsible for Justice and Compassion.
With His creativity and compassion,
Jesus calls us to be God's Words and Children.
Spirituality is Laughter, Newness, Joy*

COMPASSION

*is not only an experience between people;
It is also an experience among people
and trees and plants,
among people and animals of all kinds,
among people and music and painting and
the arts,
among people and
God.*

Christian Vitality

<u>Awakened in Faith</u>
*A proximate immediate means of Union
with God
rooted in the deepest domain of man,
well below the senses.*

<u>Celebration of Life</u>
*Celebrate Gift of Life, Gift of Creation
Festivity
Joy, Celebration which needs Sacrifice
The Feast demands the Fast*

<u>Sensuousness</u>
*Mystical Life; Total Human response to
Mystery is Sensuous*

<u>Freedom</u>
*Spontaneity and Universal Kinship
The inability to keep Love alive
is the most culpable human crime.*

Christian Mysticism

*Not tripping out,
but standing in*

*Not an introvert,
but deeply immersed in the world.*

Mysticism not taught, it's caught.

Mystic FEELS the presence of God.

Man has been reduced to a mine-machine.

*We must risk security and certainty and
Suffer our way
into a rich rewarding experience of life.*

*The experience of Nothing (Nada)
lies at the heart of a Spiritual Life.*

Four Horsemen of the Apocalypse
(Four elements of human nature)

<u>Pale Horse (Calf, Ox, Bull)</u>
Physical Body, Material Things
Gospel of Matthew

<u>Red Horse (Eagle)</u>
Emotion, Feelings
Gospel of Luke

<u>Black Horse (Man)</u>
Intellect, Thoughts
Gospel of Mark

<u>White Horse (Lion)</u>
Realization of Presence of God
Gospel of John

*We are here to learn the Truth of Being,
to learn to become Self-conscious
Self-governed entities,
Focal Points of the Divine Mind,
each expressing God in a new way.
Love of God is the answer to every problem.
All sins, troubles, sickness, poverty,
and even death
are the result of the want of Love of God.
All heath, success, prosperity, beauty, joy,
happiness
consist in Loving God.*

The Native American Talking Stick

Only the one who holds the stick may speak.
(No one is to step on his sharing.)
What is said is to be important,
significant to him.
(No trivia)
He may speak about himself,
about his own feelings.
(It is OK to share how others make him feel.)
What he says must be Truthful
and from the Heart.
(No Masks)
He should be concise, brief.
(Get to the heart of the matter.)
The stick is passed around the circle,
never across.
(Responses to others' sharings in not required.)
(One may pass the stick on without speaking.)

NATURAL EMOTIONS

FEAR
Natural: Falling, Loud Noises
Unnatural: All other fears

ANGER
Natural: 15 seconds long
Unnatural: Focused at people, Used to Harm

GRIEF
Come to grips with all the losses in Life.

JEALOUSY
Natural: Stimulus to Grow
Unnatural: Competition

LOVE
Holding, Hugging, Cuddling
Tough Love: Saying No

HEALING

A lifelong journey toward Wholeness

*Remembering what has been forgotten about
Connection, Unity, Interdependence
among all things, living and non-living*

Embracing what is most feared

Opening what has been closed

*Softening what has been hardened
into an obstruction*

*Entering into
the Transcendent Timeless Moment*

Creativity, Passion, Love

Seeking and then Expressing Self

Learning to Trust Life

You cannot negate what is not there.
That which is unborn in you can never die.
Contemplation releases it.
What feels like negation and loss is really
a liberation from a falsified consciousness,
a liberation in which nothing is lost,
except that which is not there,
a liberation where nothing is gained,
except an awakening to
what always is.

*Science
may be able to add some years to my life,
but ultimately it's up to me to*

Add some Life to my years.

I am determined to see.

I am determined to see things differently.

*Blessed is he who is
too busy in the daytime
and too sleepy at night
to worry.*

GIVING
is the secret of a healthy life.
Not necessarily money,
but whatever one has of
ENCOURAGEMENT, SYMPATHY,
UNDERSTANDING.

PRAYER:

*The un-diapered child
beneath the Maternal gaze.*

After you have listened to all the Masters,

wash out your ears

and be Silent.

There is no otherness.

*Only the child
whose mouth is empty
receives the Mother's milk.*

GARDENING

*is actively participating
in the
deepest mysteries of the Universe.*

*What happens to another,
whether it be a joy or sorrow,
happens to me.
Another's pain is my pain;
my pain is others' pain.
To relieve another's pain
is to relieve one's own
and the pain of God
who shares in all the pain in the Universe.*

Jesus can come to us in five ways at Mass

*In the Eucharist
(His Body and Blood for us)*

*In the Word
(His Message of Life for us)*

*Through the Minister
(His designated minister for us)*

*Through our brothers and sisters around us
(Even those who are late or who talk)*

*Through the Music
(However good or bad it may be)*

*You may rarely hit all five; two or three are great.
But when you hit all five:*

ZINGO!

*Worry not about each brush stroke,
about each note, about each word,
about each minute.*

*Let the beautiful painting,
the wonderful song, the marvelous poem,
the glorious life
that is within you
come out in Praise and Thanks to God.*

Regarding the Question:
Whom do I need to Love more?
Myself? (God in me?)
Others? (God in others?)

The answer is:
The question is inappropriate.
Love is non-measurable, non-quantifiable,
non-comparable.

I need to Love myself as God Loves me.
I need to Love God in others.
And True Love is not exclusive;

True Love is Inclusive.

A bell to be a bell must be rung.
A song to be a song must be sung.
God gave us Love, not in our Hearts to stay,
for Love to be Love must be Given away.

*Go where he will, the Wise man is at home,
His hearth the earth,
His hall the azure dome.
Where his clear Spirit leads him,
There's his road
By God's own light
illumined and foreshadowed.*

JUSTICE
Treating people as they deserve

MERCY
Treating people better than they deserve

*To the Attentive eye,
each moment of the year
has its own beauty
and
in the same field,
it beholds every hour a picture which
was never seen before
and which
will never be seen again.*

Hey prospective artists,
worried about being able to paint well?
Self-conscious?
Follow my lead; Paint My Sky.
No symmetry, no pattern;
most colors in most combinations go.
All shapes, sizes, forms, techniques work.
No two are alike.
It can be changed – and is – again and again.
The possibilities are endless.
No one can say it's not original.
And mistakes – smudges, smears, slips
all look normal.
So go ahead; Paint My Sky.

*One thing is sure:
Man today must be obsessed;
if he is, there is still Hope.
If he is Passionate, meaning Com-passionate,
there is, indeed, Hope.*

*In the face of suffering
one has no right to turn away, not to see.
In the face of injustice,
one may not look the other way.
When someone suffers, and it is not you,
he comes first.
His very suffering gives him priority.
To watch over another person who grieves
is a more urgent duty than to think of God.*

MYSTICISM

*Experience, Non-dualism, Compassion,
Making Connection, Awe,
Affirmation of the world as a whole,
Right Brain, Self-critical,
Heart Knowledge,
Return to the Source, Feminine,
Silence, Nothingness, Darkness,
Childlike Playfulness,
Psychic Justice,
Prophetic, Being with Being,
True Self,
Globally, Cosmically Ecumenical*

EDUCATION

I used to think Education
(Lt. Educere: To Lead out)
meant
To Lead the Student out of
the darkness of ignorance.
I now believe it means
To Lead out of each of us
the Gift that is the Mystic within.

GATHERING OF MEN

*To help our Spiritual growth,
we come together in a non-hierarchical,
non-elective
Gathering
devoted to fostering the development of
our True Christian Male Identity.
In a group of eight to ten men,
we meet regularly
to Share our thoughts, feelings, and
experiences,
to Nurture and Support each other,
and to Develop and Grow Spiritually
in a variety of new positive directions.
We strive to be
Warm, Loving, Open, Sensitive and
Cooperative,
while Nurturing and Supporting each other
and the other men, women and children in
our lives.*

*We reject
the rigid and destructive traditional male role
which requires men to be tough, aggressive,
competitive,
while suppressing emotions
and being insensitive to the feelings of others,*

*proving manhood by domination and intimidation.
We are committed to being free
of this stereotyped male role
helping each other to be more
Christ-like.*

Perspective
(Two men looked out from prison bars . . .)
The sailboat sat resting on its hoist,
when a tiny bird landed on its mast.
"What a Blessing, What Luck!" he said,
"It'll probably shit on your boat," said she.
(. . . One saw mud, the other stars.)

GATHERING OF MEN
Whenever men find themselves in a situation
safe enough
to allow their feelings to become conscious,
they descend
and the waters rise up and flow out
to all those present,
reconnecting them to each other
and to the cyclical stages of life.
Through these rituals of descent, men can find
emotional connections among the generations
that remind us that
besides the fires that can threaten and divide,
there is the Water of Life
that can flow into and fill the gaps
that always occur
between generations, genders, races, cultures,
persons.

*Write the wrongs that are done to you
in sand.
Write the good things that happen to you
on a piece of marble.
Let go of all emotions such as resentment and
retaliation,
which only diminish you.
Hold on to emotions such as
Gratitude and Joy
which increase you.*

Prayer

Amen.

*. . . the Adventure
is just beginning . . .*

Made in the USA